LUMMOX Press

These poems are an explosion of Joe's truth in a lying world. I know Joe—I don't know how but I always saw the great man and broken boy hidden behind the gruff, sarcastic, self-deprecating tough exterior Joe put on for the world. I guess that is why I find him in a new place every few years and we talk via email or text OR the evil Facebook messenger. Joe is in a great place now, with a family that loves him in all his brokenness.

Finally poetry can be a release for the everyman. How does a man speak? I mean the hard man, the man that has seen things—things from hell that most couldn't handle and things from Heaven that most still couldn't handle. A man that hears his demons scream and can face them in all of their intensity. Well this book of poetry is how Joe speaks. These poems are cries against the night, cries for mercy from the pain and forever the struggle of the ones unwilling to surrender to the fate that is.

—Drew Ishmael

Joe's a dedicated and curious man. He's also a realist, and as such he can't help but be a cynic (especially in this day and age). He wants things to work, to know why things stop working and how to fix them (because he KNOWS just as sure as the sun rises, that SOMEONE will break it). Joe has a pretty good idea who that SOMEONE is but he has no hard evidence and this frustrates him to no end.

When you read his poetry, you will "hear" this frustration in his poetic voice. You can't miss it; it's in a lot of his poems. It is, perhaps the voice of a generation of frustrated kids, hungry for something...more, something intangible, something overlooked, some *thing*. It is! This is your own MORAL OUTRAGE. So sit back, hang on tight and get ready for an adventure.

—*Rd Armstrong*

IN THE SHADOW
OF THE BOMB

J. W. Gardner

ISBN 978-1-929878-68-0

First edition

LUMMOX Press

PO Box 5301
San Pedro, CA 90733
www.lummoxpress.com

Printed in the United States of America

TABLE OF CONTENTS

PART 1: THE SAN JOAQUIN VALLEY

PART 2: ELKWD

PART 3: '93 TO THE FALLING TOWERS

PART 4: 9 YEARS ADRIFT

PART 5: 20 YEARS LATER

IN THE SHADOW
OF THE BOMB

"Why don't you paint me a sunset?"

—Lee Gardner 1949-2008

This book is the sunset I painted for you, Dad.

You never know what words of wisdom are going to carry with you over the years. I was about 14, and was just starting to show my efforts at writing and drawing/painting. It was terrible stuff really.

I really didn't know anything about poetry at the time. That's not meant to imply that I know anything about poetry today, either.

Back then I was reading a lot of Lovecraft, Blake, and a little bit of Whitman and Poe. Pretty much I was just trying to write rock songs and my big idea of clever was to filter it through generic macabre imagery. You know... Jim Morrison. Except I can't sing; so I started calling it poetry.

You know...Jim Morrison.

Anyways, I was showing all this "art" to my old man, when he tells me, "Why don't you paint me a sunset? Write to me about a dog finally coming up on some good luck? Give me something I can find identity in, something I can understand. Tell me about living a real life."

At first I was all about my teenager hurt feelings. But the seed was planted, the ember smoldering, if you will. I was 16 when me and the pen got together again. This time I was trying to write about what I knew. Turns out, at 16 I didn't know much at all.

Now, here I am, 40 years old and I'm repeating my father's words; trying to tell you what this is all about.

I write about what I know.

I write about the last 40 years of life I've seen.

See, the thing is, it don't matter what I meant when I was writing it. Really, it comes down to just one question.

What does it mean to you?

PART 1:

THE
SAN JOAQUIN
VALLEY

THE END OF THE GRAPEVINE

It's not far

But it may as well be another world.

You take the 5 north
Through LA
On out past Magic Mountain
Snake the slow climb
Up the Grapevine

Lumbering big truck column
On the right
Like the ancient dinosaurs
Burning in shining stainless steel fuel tanks
Saddle strapped to the sides

Come up to Bakersfield
Home of that sound
And Buck Owens
Keep pushing through
Shift to the 99

Get comfortable   and take your time
Watch the march of progress
Fly by in the left lane

Followed by big CHP cruisers
And redneck country boy pickup
Jacked up bruisers

Pastures

On both sides filled
With migrant field
Workers
Far from the big city glitz and glamour
Places with names like
Turlock
Knight's Ferry
Truckee
Modesto
Ceres
Empire
Riverbank
Escalon and Farmington...
Yea now we walk through the shadow of the San Joaquin Valley

THE FIRST HOUSE

The first house
I remember knowing as home
Looked like a Norman Rockwell painting
Of a drug induced hell.

Built in the twenties
An old farmhouse
Shifted slightly sideways
Slow decline off its foundation.

The fields have long turned their last plows
They lay rusted dead hulks
Where they were last drawn
Stable barns of rotten wood
Charred from some forgotten fire
Quarter mile dirt strip to the main hi-way
To find the mail box
Or the early morning school bus
Or go cart race car fantasy
Of being Mario Andretti
Catching black widows in a jar
Or gopher snakes as pets
Oil lanterns at night
And big pitchers of Kool-Aid
Hot dogs and Mac-N-Cheese on good days
And it was all just living.

KEEP UP

The only grandfather I ever knew
Was Mr. Paul Wieber
United States Army (retired)
He stood six foot six
I was maybe round his knee bout this time.

Every morning he would go for his walks...

His legs would stride out long
The ground passing beneath
His feet like running water

I don't know if he'll be able to keep up
He said
       I'll keep up
I said

And we would walk
Miles would disappear
I learned how to step it out
And keep pace with him.
There was never a lot of talking
Just the walk

I held his hand
The day the ambulance came and took him away

I never saw him again

It was a large funeral
Many many respectable people showed up
A letter from the President
21 gun salute
That still strikes
The drum of my heart
Marking the time
As I still step it out
And keep pace
Like he taught me

CHILDHOOD HEROES

They looked like Vikings
These monsters disguised
In the flesh
Of men
Like northern nightmare remnants
Roaming the hard lands
Dressed in furs and leathers

On hips
Were blades and hammers
And tucked away were always guns
Of various calibers.

These wild men
Far roamers
These Easy Riders
On their Iron Horses
Were my first heroes

Their flesh marked with scars
And arcane tattoos
Big silver rings
Fashioned as skulls
Fat chains holding fatter wallets
Leather gauntlets
And heavy boots
Capped in steel

Always at the Gatherings
These round ups of rebels
Were the roaring of Harleys
And old Fords and Chevys
Barrels of beer
And half naked women all around

It was during this time
That I found my hunger
To be wild
To be free
To be like these savages

Answering to no man

THE PARK

I always called it the park
Or later the sticks
Not real certain what its actual name was

We also knew it as
Moose Park
La Loma Park
And
Dry Creek Park
Which is a strange name
As my mother will attest
That park was anything but dry

From 2 to 12 years old
        That park was home
It was safe
I was a modern Huck Finn
And that little creek like a river was my only constant friend.

I watched a whole generation rise and fall
Like sand castle empires there.
I remember the park people
The Carsons, Old Crazy Joe Riley
Too Tall Paul, Rodger Podger
A giant dog named George
And so many more...

Guitars strumming and harmonicas honking
Kids off key making words up to sing along
BBQ grills flaring, dogs barking
Soft ball games and the constant worry of bee stings
Beer in the cooler

And look around
You'll find a burning number...

GI Joe wars along the creek
Soon
Became pellet gun
And
Dirt clod wars
Running
Like a dog through the sticks
Splashing through the cricks
No streetlight
To mimic mommas warning
Watch the sun
Follow its ark
Through the trees
Get home
Before the birds quit singing

That park was a place of beginnings
Had my first cigarette
And beer there
Smoked my first joint
And
Kissed a girl there
For the first time...

And so many
Long days afterwards
Spent
Pondering existence.

RAT FATE

The rats
At Dry Creek Park
Would get big as a large tom cat
And as bold as a dog.

Every so often one
Would come running
To the sandbox.

That was always quite the festival
Kids screaming parents running
Dogs barking
Everyone chasing this goddamned
King Kong rat around...

Most times
The rat would make it back
To the creek
Lost in the warren
Of twisted trunks and roots
And sewers.

Other times
The groundskeepers
Would come out with their litter sticks
And skewer
The rat.

They would wiggle their fat bodies
About halfway up the shaft
Before finally giving up the last breath.

I still remember watching that
And being told
That's the fate of all rats.

PAYING RENT

Modesto 1978
On the wrong side of the tracks
Other side of Yosemite

Airport District

Built in the 1930s
First for
Dust Bowl migrant Oakies
Then later
Mexican migrant farm workers...

Overflowing ancient septic tanks
No sewers, no sidewalks, no streetlights
No building permits, no code inspectors
Housed in houses without foundations
No voice, no say, no one would listen anyway

Now overwhelmed
By walking dead addicts and drunks
And the hardscrabble children
Fighting over the bones
Of last night's carnage

And it's been like this
Generation
After
Generation
Of struggling
Dirt nasty daily fight for survival...

Everybody trying to scratch out a living
Rabbit hutches and mean vegetable gardens
Replaced with meth houses and desperation

If mama has to pay the rent
Is it still prostitution?

MAILBOX

A lonely mailbox
At the end of a dirt road
Only connection to the outside world
     A sacred and worshiped spot

Hidden in the fields
Like a cat
Stalking birds
Only a whisper I move as a shadow
Watching for the mailman
Ears
Straining
To hear
The grinding
Gears
Of his jeep

Watching that mailbox
Ready to pounce
Should that jeep stop.

CROSSING GAURD

In 1984 I was a student crossing guard
At Wilson Elementary school.
I had it all
Orange safety vest and hard hat
Wooden stop sign and whistle around my neck.

There was a small sense of wonder at the power I held
I determined when cars drove and when walkers walked
I determined who passed the crosswalk...

I got beat up a lot that year.

Funny how things change but stay the same
But somehow still seem to go away.

I don't know, one day it's all right there
And then in the hustle of it all
The Army, two failed marriages, the booze
And always, always chasing my thoughts with my pen

I don't know, somehow I quit noticing
Then pretty soon I quit noticing
That I didn't notice...

And then they're gone

Like telephone booths and drive in theatres
And early lessons in civic responsibility.

NOTHING TO HEAR

Sometimes it is everything I can do
To keep these feelings blunted
Sharp edges rolled and wrapped
Soaked in booze and smoke
And crushed up pain pills

No I don't want to talk about it
Don't want any inventory
No 4th step confessions
It was bad enough
The first time
No I don't want to re-live it
Re-visit it inspect it
Search it high and low
Get to the root of it

I know the answer
Always had the common denominator
To unlock that complex combination lock
Holding my iron mask in place

Yes I had a bad day
Again
Same kind of day as was yesterday
Just leave me alone
I'll sort it out
It's just more of the same anyways

Nothing new nothing changed
Another day getting my ass kicked at school
Made fun of for my high-water
Husky Tuff Skins Kmart Jeans
With the patches on the knees
And dime store shoes
That don't even got any stripes on the side

And when I come home
Everyone is always so mad at me
Cause my clothes are torn and dirty
And my lip is swollen again
Just like yesterday

And everyone tells me not to fight
Even had my dad come up from LA
To tell me not to fight

And no one would hear
Everyone talking so much about how
All my fighting
Is making them feel
All about their feelings
But mine won't be heard

Nothing to say
Wouldn't matter anyway
So why bother to say anything

So now when I come home
Everyone is still so mad at me
Everything still torn dirty and bloody
Except for my knuckles
And my pride
Got good at taking
The best ass whooping
In three towns
Hands stuffed deep in my pockets
To keep from swinging
Teeth clenched on the collar of my shirt
To keep from biting
Just so I can come home
And say I wasn't fighting

So no
I don't want to talk about it
Don't want to discuss
How at school
It's so very cool
To shit on me
Even the teachers
Get in on it
Can't walk across campus
Without having to deal with the constant
Nerve rending harassment
Even the girls are getting in on it

Get together and sing along
"We got a dog named Joe
He's got the healthy Hi-Pro Glow
Hi-Pro Alpo for the low slow dog Joe"

And the teachers
All say I'm stupid
"Kid don't even know his last name"
"What's wrong with him?"
"He thinks his father lives in LA"

So no I don't want to talk about it
Don't want to work through it
Don't want to think about it
There is nothing to deal with
Other than blunting these feelings
Sharp edges rolled and wrapped
Soaked in booze and smoke
And crushed up pain pills...

COLLISION

Now that the rain has begun to fall
The river swollen pregnant
With debris rushing out to the sea
So swift and furious
Momentum built from the mountain
Falling with gravity and purity
A collision
Blinds the days with a watery haze
That conceals moments
Of reckoning or wrecking
In a man's life…

Father
Forgive my cowardice…
Mother
Forgive my arrogance…

The dust would puff up
Like little atomic explosions
As I would scuff my sneakers
Along the dirt driveway
Like a condemned man walking
His last walk
Slow and stuttering each step
To the school bus stop
Waiting for the grinding of gears
And the perfume of diesel exhaust
To herald the beginning
Of another day of torture.

Yesterday I was taught an important lesson
About
      FAIRNESS
And
REALITY

So today I brought a brick in my book bag
And a roll of nickels
Wrapped in black electrical tape
Like I saw my father do with a roll of quarters
Before he would go out
To do his night time work…

AT FIRST A BLESSING

Grilled cheese sandwiches
And
Tomato soup
Endless days of the stuff.

At first a blessing
A bounty
Eyes
Filled with gratitude
When we
Got all them white label cans
Bread
And blocks of cheese.

After while
It got to where
The
Painful grumbling
In our bellies was
Preferable
To grilled cheese sandwiches
And
Tomato soup

MRS. ROSE

She worked hard

Hard as she was
Hard like carbon
Buried at the bottom
Of the Earth's mantle
Hard as a diamond

To wash
The gutter
Taint
Of aint
Outta my mouth

She was the first teacher
I ever had
That cared
About the end result
Of her efforts

Little pontoon boat
On a string
Sink your ship
Every time you let the tongue slip
With some bullshit
Talking "aint"
Like it aint got no taint

4/5th grade class
She was my teacher
She had taught
My step father
And his best friend Abner
Back in their day

Now
Today
They all bowl on the same league
Down at the Yosemite Lanes
On the proper side of the railroad tracks

She would always tell me
A man is limited
Only
By his vocabulary

The cut of your cloth
Will be measured
By your ability
To express yourself

Enunciate
Announce
Pronounce
Be heard

STOMACHACHE

Practice the lies in the mirror
Careful inspection
Insure there will be no detection
Of the fear
That sleeps there

Deep thoughts
Invested
To explain
Why my stomach is always in pain
Anger and stress poorly digested

Head down eyes always on the move
Another new school with the same rules
Always ready for the foot kicked out in the aisle
Lunch tray knocked outta hands
Books took torn apart
Papers with hand written stories of revenge
Thrown tossed to the wind
Circled around
Kicked down
To the ground
Again

IN THE SHADOW OF THE BOMB

We never had a chance...
An entire generation raised
By grandparents and the state

Television taught us
Reading writing math and morality
Sesame St. Electric Co. 321 Contact
Capt. Kangaroo and Mr. Green Jeans
Romper Room, please call my name!
And God keep him well
Mr. Rodgers.

Children in the shadow of the Bomb
While our parents
Like summer grasshoppers
Squandered our future away
Pledge of Allegiance and bomb drills
"The Russians are coming!"
On a failing wave of
Domino Theory Communism
And the Berlin Wall
Still stood ugly and tall...

All hyped up after watching Red Dawn
At the theatre with fathers and uncles
Screaming WOLVERINES
As we ran through the park
Gathered around the television glow to watch the Day After
When we still wanted to be
Fire fighters and astronauts...
We never had a chance
Watching the Challenger explode 5th grade
With our house key around our necks

To come to empty home
To watch more TV when sitcoms were funny...

ReRun pop locking
On What's Happening
Happy Days and an alien named Mork
MASH and Sanford and Son

And primetime was for adults...
But if you were good and quiet
Maybe you'd get to watch
Some Hill St. Blues
Or catch a bit of Miami Vice
If you were really lucky.

Saturday mornings were
Cartoons, Combat and Kung Fu Theatre

And always
Moving on up
Were the Jeffersons
And the Bunkers
All in the Family...

Do you remember when George and Archie met?
Remember
How they showed us
We really weren't that different?
Do you remember
Your house key around your neck?
Do you remember
When we had a chance?

IDIOT WISDOM

P.O.S. Maverick
Painted with brushes
Suitcase latches
Holding the roof in place
Three on the tree
1st gear don't engage
Four bald tires and no spare
No jack no star
Just a bent rusty screwdriver
Stuck in the ignition
Rolling down the country road
Going to the country store
Going to use the telephone
Going to get some change
On the food stamps
Cash in the cans in the trunk of the Maverick
To get some sodas and beer
Maybe a pack of Kool King Cigarettes
Heading back to cinderblock cube called home
Nestled between a cow pasture and rice paddy
Crossed by giant endless horizon to horizon
Corn fields filled
With wise and cruel magical scarecrows
Holding court
Endlessly laughing mocking

Taking
Such glee
In our misery
Always there whispering in the wind
There is no escape
No escape
Like the rabbit in the jaws of the wolf
Field mouse in the curved raptor's talon
The secrets of idiot wisdom

MY FRIEND WITH THE GUITAR

Old Crazy Joe Riley
Died the other day.

Along with him went
A great treasure
Of my childhood.

See
Old Crazy Joe Riley
Was a junkie and a bum with a guitar

And he was my friend.

He'd strum that old guitar
That was never far
From him
He'd smoke a little weed
Drink some beer
And play some Lynard Skynard tunes

That was about the speed of life
For Old Crazy Joe Riley

I didn't know what heroin was back then
But he knew all about smack

Old Crazy Joe Riley
Could be
A willfully
Stubborn man
When pushed

He kept his principles
And his bicycle
But the young park tuffs
Broke his back and neck
When they threw
Him and his bike
Off the bridge in La Loma Park
Where I spent my childhood days
Long before the park
Ever heard of Lacy Peterson
Or Chandra Levy

Back when the Airport District
Was just working poor rough
And not a shanty row of meth houses

This was in Modesto CA
In 1980
Before seatbelt laws
And
Compact parking spaces
And
Cell phones
And
Internet
And
Video games
Were mostly playing
The Oregon Trail at school
On old green screen Apple computers

And
Merle Haggard would still come through town
And
We were the last generation
To grow up under the Shadow of the Bomb
And
We still did the pledge of allegiance
Before doing our bomb drills
Which after while
Became earthquake drills
Where you curled under your desk
So the searchers
Would be able to find
Your remains

Like they found
Old Crazy Joe Riley
With a guitar
And a needle in his arm

NODDING TO OZ

I was about ten
Maybe 12
When
The day came
And he said
To me

Only two kind of men

Pimps
And
Johns...

As the strap
Slid off his arm

As the heroin
Took him

The drool running down his chin

Leading to the poppy path of Oz
East to the Land of Nod

I knew he meant
What he said
By the
Big silver and turquoise
Rings
On all fingers
And the two
Crisp brand new
Twenties
He gave me
To watch over him
While he was in the Nod...

FLYING BACK THEN

It was maybe
In the 5th grade
The first time I ever
Traveled by plane.

Back then
All the seats
Had armrests
With ashtrays built in them
And all the flight attendants
Were beautiful women
That you called
STEWARDESS

Normally
I would be the only kid
And all these beautiful women
Who always smelled so
NICE
Would tend to me like
ROYALTY
Extra soda pops and peanuts

Always midway through the flight
The
BIG DEAL
Would happen

The
CAPTAIN
Would send the
Beautiful pretty smelling
STEWARDESS
To bring me to the
COCKPIT
To relieve the
CAPTAIN.
Headphones on my ears
The flight stick in my hands
And the
CO-PILOT
Would say
Command of the plane is all yours
CAPTAIN JOE
And there I was
Big as shit
Ten years old
Flying a jet airplane.

After a bit the
CAPTAIN
Would return to the
COCKPIT
Shake my hand and tell me I did a good piece of flying

And then
He would pin a set of
WINGS
To my chest

And I would return to my seat
Buckle in
And prepare for landing

Grinning ear to ear
Hand over my heart
Clutching those silver
WINGS
Knowing that I could do anything now...

Hell
I just flew a jet.

FORWARD MOVEMENT

You put
One foot in front of another
And do
It again and again

Head down eyes cast aside
No direction
No destination

Just the forward movement
Of putting one down
Picking the other up
Do it again and again

It's just like what's for dinner
Chicken tonight
Feathers tomorrow
And prayers
For the rest of the week

You put one foot in front of another
Pick one up put one down
Need some get some
Got some leave some
And no ones left hungry
Just forward movement

Pick 'em up
Put 'em down
Eyes up and steady
No direction
No destination
Just forward movement.

PART 2:
ELKWD

TRAIN TICKET

It used
To just be
A bench
And ticket stand
What passed for
The Amtrak station
In Riverbank

I used to hop
The train there
Every summer
Make my way to LA.

6 hours on the train
Sneaking smokes
Between the cars
Watching
CENTRAL
CALIFORNIA
Roll by the windows

Weather beaten barns
And
Old farm equipment
Whose names
And use
Are
Lost
To another age

Grape vines
And

Fields of corn
Small dusty towns
And
General stores
Two lane roads
That follow
The tracks
And the water
All the way to
Bakersfield

Transfer to a bus
Now the
Windows show
The passing
GRAPEVINE
MOUNTAIN ROAD
Filled with cars
Unending stream

Past Magic Mountain
Dropping
Like
Cholesterol
Into the heart
Of LA

Union Station
Huge
Granite and marble
Monument to a grander age

GOODMORNING

She closes her eyes
Gentle salty sighs
Drawing softly her ocean shades
Over my city
While the slow glow
Slowly grows
In the eastern skies
Early morning sunrise
Full of promise and surprise

LAKEWOOD OAKIE

I live here, this is my home

This was the home
Of my fathers before me

Back when the family
Came here to escape
The Dust Bowl nightmare
Great Depression misery
2nd generation American
Dirty barefoot Oakie trash
Go back go back go back
Border state bastards
Go back

No room for us here
No hope for us there
No chicken in the pot
No pot to squat and piss in
Nothing to do
But survive the
GOLDEN YEAR TO CALIFORNIAN CITIZENSHIP

Pick fruit all the way down the valley
Make the way
To the coast
Work the docks lumberyards
Aero-space union fed jobs
Get up good come up quick
Buy a home in the world's first
Sub-division

Shopping centers and schools
River regulated by Army Corps of Engineers
Lots of Navy work and Navy boys
Spending Navy dollars
Grand influence to economy driving
Like Cal Worthington
Back then
Till he died
Carrying his own paper
Putting everyone behind the wheel
Of The American Dream,
A big V8 roaring along the new freeways of modern
inspiration connecting everyone
And everything to the Promised Land
For the Greatest Generation

WALK ALONE

Walk alone
Was the advice
My old man gave me

Words of wisdom
Hard earned on the streets
 And prison

He tried to give to me
The only thing of value he had

His lifetime
Of scars and tattoos
A broken road map
Marked with care

There be dragons
Bad water   long desert
Stay away   no good

Listen closely son
Don't do the things I've done

SUMMER OF RAMIREZ

1985
One hot mother
Of a summer
Windows and doors
Left open
Sweltering
The heat
Driving everyone crazy
City
Gripped with fear
Sweating
As one crazed beast
While the Night Stalker
Was out
Hunting the streets

DON'T CHASE

Juan and his brother
I don't remember his name either
Lived at the end of Corby
Me at the other end
Right next to the park.

We got into
Some sort of disagreement
Or another that turned to harsh words
For 12 year olds...

My father saw me chasing Juan
And his brother down the street

My father came after me
Belt licking fire through the air...

He ran me back down the street
A public display of a whipping
No words shouted
Just the language of leather
And the sacrament of my young tears
And confusion.

Later
That night
He explained to me…

You can't chase them boy
Just bide your time
And they will get theirs…

Juan and his brother
Found out about
The child molester
At their end of the block.

Sorry about your luck Juan
You should've run faster.

TROUBADOUR

I like the feel of night time grass
Brushing beneath my feet
Sneaking between my toes…

We reminded each other of Hollywood 1989
At the Troubadour
Underage

I swung on the lead singer
     I was lucky to get out alive

I never had felt so alive

As I did on the ride back
In the back
Of Pat's pickup
       You snuggled close to me
       I spread my leather like a blanket
       Over us
As we hurtled back to Lakewood

MI AMORES

It was a little mom and pop pizza joint
On the corner of Del Amo
And Pioneer in East Lakewood.
The owner, Al
Gave me a job there
When I was 14
Washing dishes
And sometimes making pizzas.
Wasn't a bad gig as far as work went for teenagers
Beat the shit outta the fields
In the San Joaquin valley
Or carrying roofing material and 2x4s
Or working at the damn McDonald's or Del Taco
And I didn't have enough sense
Or concern
To get on with one of the grocery stores.
Like I said it wasn't a bad gig
There was always the free meal
At the end of the shift
And of course we hit
The beer taps as well.
It was outside that joint
When Sebastian stuck a gun in my face
And my buddy Monty put a knife to his neck
And I kept laughing
I was so drunk I didn't know the danger I was in

That's when I realized that nothing
Ever
Was going to be as perfect as that moment
Until it was over
And the next moment began
Like when Al
Caught me making out with a girl
In the restroom of his restaurant
Being told to get a room
This aint no cess pit
And I couldn't stop laughing
Cause it was at that moment
Right then and there
That I realized
None of it really matters

FRESHMAN YEAR ARTESIA HIGH SCHOOL

I spent
Most of high school
Drunk

I was in love
With the romance
Of the drunken writer

I wanted
The grand adventure
Of Hemingway and Chinaski
I wanted the dark nature
The mysterious allure

Mostly
I just wanted
To get through the day
Without having
To deal with anybody

At school there were very
Distinct
Groups

And either you
Were in
Or you
Were not.

By the library

You had
All the long hairs
And stoners
The rock n roll
And heavy metal crowd

By the bell

All the athletes
And brains
All those going places kids

Down from there

Were the Asian kids
As mysterious
As an abacus

And then
The small Goth crowd
Their misery didn't need much company

Out by the metal and auto shop
Like a bad stereotype
Were the Hispanic kids

And then there was them

Jay H

Chris M

Real punk rock kids
Mohawks and Docs
Bad attitudes
And not liked by anyone

But everyone knew them

Stayed away from them

Left them alone

Just the way they liked it

So of course
It became important
For me
To have them
Not like me
Cause then
I'd be even cooler
Than I thought they were

LLOYDS PETS

At the corners
Of 25 years ago
Pioneer and Centralia
Next to the donut shop
That's been there forever
Along the side of OK Liquor
Was about the coolest place
A 14 year old boy
Could find to hang out.
Snakes and Monitors
Of all shape size and color.

After being kicked out of Comics Unlimited
On Norwalk Blvd two blocks into the Gardens
For reading and not buying
We would cut
Across Centralia
And go to Lloyds Pets.

Sometimes we would get lucky
And get to watch
The big ones eat rabbits and rats.

One day they had something new on display
A true abomination
That still haunts
The primate brain instincts
Worse than any of the reptiles

This armored demon
Showed me the True Face of Fear
It was so very majestic in its terror
It stood up in its glass prison
Hissing loudly
This King Cockroach

ROCK CLIMBING

Joshua Tree
Stonbraker and Noble
Always at the helm
Always on belay.

40 some tough suburban kids
From Artesia High school
Out in the desert
Some for the first time
Out in Nature

Sometimes
I remember
The names

Mike, Ruth, Jenni

Sometimes I remember
The faces

Mostly I just remember
Belonging.

A weekend in the desert
Climbing rock faces
Like Baby's Butt
Hiking Upper and Lower Grotto
Marking constellations
In the obsidian sky
And for that one weekend
All the pretensions
Were swept aside
And we were all
Human.

2 COUNTS OF FELONY ASSAULT

Los Padrinos Juvenile Court
16 and so very unaware
Of the enormity
Of the
Charges
I was faced with
2 counts of felony assault with a deadly weapon
With the intent to do great bodily harm
Print ink stained fingers
Bracelets behind my back
Led in chains like a dog
My father's face creased with worry
So afraid that his past sin
Passed to his misbegotten son

A 5'7, 130 pound book worm
Declared by the DA
Danger to society
Unbalanced
Prone to violent outbursts
Recommendation for confinement
For a term of no less than five years

So very unaware
Of what it all meant
Looking at my father
My smile full of youth
I did the right thing
I chased them boys away from my sister

Ricky and James never came back again
Not even to testify

My smile fixed I watched the judge
Erupt in anger
At having his court time wasted
Charges dropped with prejudice to the State
Unshackled
The DA says
We will be
Watching you
You will be back
Father telling me
Don't look back son
Don't ever look back...

MARKS THE SPOT

He had earrings and long hair
Tattoos
Crawled like oily serpents
Along his skinny scarred arms.

A cigarette in his mouth
Always lit
Another one behind his ear
Waiting to be called to order.

Rocks in his socks
And a pint of schnapps
Stashed in his back pocket.

Leather biker jacket
Adorned
With chains and patches and spikes.

Worn like proud street knight armor
Four inch folding stiletto sabre
Tucked up the right sleeve.

She hangs at his side
Always there with too much make up
And that teased up
Aqua Rock Hair.

Clothes tight to show
What could be had tonight
One kid with the state
Another on the way.

Powder rings
Around nostrils
Tattoo of a flying heart
On her chest
Hoping one day
It'll find a place to rest.

Vagabond children of the streets
Baby Boomers ignored burden

Gen X Marks
The spot
Of the Lost

MURDER OF CROWS

I remember
Softly

On the roofs
On the wires

Along the fences
And the street signs

Every limb and branch
All rustle black
With these heralds
Of the One Eyed Father

Murders of crows
All of Lakewood
Silently watched
By obsidian eyes

Then
As if from some mysterious
Commune
As one
The great cawing
Choir
Of carrion eaters
Would take to wing
A great blackened storm cloud
Of
Beak
And
Talon
And
Feather

EAST LAKEWOOD ROYALTY

There are two street names
I remember
Back
From my neighborhood
Back
From days when I was much younger

Names
That were sometimes
Said in whisper

Pope and Spider

Real bad dogs
The stories would say
Hang out on the corners
Wrapped in black leathers
They were LADS
They were LKWD Punks
They were LKWD Stoners
Or so
The stories would go

One could set you up with some ink
To represent
That EastSide Pride
The other could settle
The trouble
No matter how it came or went

But I can't tell you
If those stories are true

I never met either one of them
I was probably too small back then

But those same stories stuck with me
They became names
That sound like East Lakewood Royalty

OLD CATS AND HUSTLE

We would creep along
A different path every time
It was all in the fun of it
It was always better with an audience
Proving it's possible

Throw the skateboard ahead
Hit the fence in a leap
One swift motion roll over the wire
Like breaking out of a labor camp

Ditching high school
School narcs
Chasing us across to Palms Park
Cut through the apartments
Hit flat pavement
With our skateboards echoing clacking
In the hallways
We were out of sight...

Circle around the school
Cut through the back neighborhoods
Rolling along 207th
Up to Pioneer
Time to decide
Run the river bed to the beach
To gawk at the girls

Or head to Cerritos Mall
To gawk at the girls
And get the mall cops to chase us

Skateboard wheels clacking on the tiled floor
Out the double doors
Hit the parking lot

And circle back around
Hang left on Artesia Blvd.
Making our way to Hard Times Billiards
On Bellflower
To watch the Old Cats
The REAL HUSTLERS
Shoot stick
And ALWAYS looking cool
Always standing in the shadows
Face lit with a glowing cigarette
And hard earned street wisdom
How we yearned to learn to be them…

THESE THINGS WERE IMPORTANT

Sitting in a garage
Tape deck spins out music
Long hair boots ripped jeans
KNAC T-shirts
Leather jackets wallet chains
Skull rings
Boys with earrings
Homemade tattoos
And Marlboros
Old Milwaukee's Best
And the occasional pinter joint.

These things were important then

Arguing
About who's better
GNR or Metallica
Sex Pistols or M.O.D.
Dead Kennedys or Black Flagg
And so many others

These things were important back then

Before jobs and taxes
And accomplice politics

Back then
It was all about what the radio would spin

GENTLE

The smoke hung
Sweet and sticky
In the air.
              We rolled another joint-
Good green bud
And passed it around
              Everything became as gentle as cotton
   So   very comfortable and warm.
We laughed all Night.

PINK

Hot wet and inviting
Young and lush
Flower with soft petals
Just blooming under my touch
Crying liquid pearls
Tart upon my tongue
      Enter

COMPLETE FAILURE

His bravado
Was
Short lived

I was surprised he had the nerve

It was a big gun...10mm

Quiet funeral
A father angry and hurt
A family forever changed

...and we told jokes about it.

BANG

This is the kid
Bullied every day at school
Beaten every day at home
For being bullied at school
Body a testimony of bruises
Mind a tortured pit of hell
Trapped in a room
With no doors
And no windows
Left alone
Twisting in the despair
No release no escape
No mercy no break
Just the constant grinding
An endless siege of the soul
While the pastor keeps saying
Trust in the Lord
Turn the other cheek
Forgive your enemies
Shivering in the cold dark of loneliness
Blind deaf mute
Suffocating on the madness
Only one way out
Only one way out
Leave me alone
Leavemealoneleavemealoneleavemealone
Enough
No more
Never again
None of you will ever hurt me again...

Bang

SELLING PAPERS

In my senior year
Of high school
I had a part time job
At the Press Telegram Newspaper
Going door to door selling subscriptions.

Wasn't a tough gig really
Once you figured the ins and outs
Of the hustle.

See back then
The newspaper was the internet
It was the hot thing
Neighbors would beat hell
Out of each other
For stealing their paper.

So the grift
Was you explain to the customer
Sign up for a year's subscription
With deferred payment for 9 months

When the bill comes due
Tell them you weren't satisfied.

I get my marks for the sell
They got their paper

And after that it was on them
To either pay the bill or not.

Most times
When the bill came
They were used to getting the paper
They went ahead and paid up
And subscribed again.

Apartments were the best

Sometimes you'd catch a whole run at once
10 15 twenty scripts
Nail two weeks numbers in an hour

And there was always the hope
For the fabled lonely wife/single mother
Nooner Hook up
That you'd read about
In the Forum section of Penthouse.

17 years old
And the whole world
Was still
A choose your own adventure novel
Left to be read

PLEASE

Please forgive me
I never meant to hurt you

Please forgive me
I just wanted to be free

Please forgive me
I have so little left to give

Please forgive me
I finally escaped.

A TROUBLED NATION

Priest
Politician
Doctor
Judge
Police
Charlatan
Salesman
Magician
Thief
Assassin
Hyphenation
Definition
Separation
Division
A troubled nation

FLOOD

The man said
Big waters a coming
Better hunker down low
Find some high ground
The waters gonna rise
And there aint no Moses
No big old ark
Someone pulled the ribbon
Of the rainbow
Undone the promise
And now the water is gonna rise
Wash away
All in the way
Deep cleansing of the land
Deep cleansing of the soul
Row for all you're worth
You lazy mongrels
Row row row
Rub a dub dub
And the boat is sinking
Glub a glub glub
And the bourbon is drinking
Chug a lug a chug
And we all are singing
And we all are marching
And we all are so merry
Falling off the edge of the world
So row row row
You drunken bastards
Row row row

PART 3:

'93 TO THE FALLING TOWERS

MILITARY

Lakewood CA; High School

Bless your feast with new thought
The radio sang soothing discordance
 Even sober it was very sublime,
 So our bodies went with the flow
Presidential campaign across a troubled nation
Desert war death
So obscene...

I came home from school to watch the war on TV
I was 16 so very naive, so very bold and daring
My patriotism
Was a hard dick
Of imagined glory
        Never knowing what a terrible price I would pay

Fort Sill Ok; Basic training and Advanced Individual training

Formation...
The cold bugle
 Shatters the glass morning
As I am broken and remade
Over and over again...

Fort Benning Georgia; Airborne Training

Today
        I get ready to enter the belly of a great bird
Carried high through the sky
The earth
So small and delicate below
Beckoning
Me to return to her dirty breast
I stood in a door
Opened
To the passing blue sky
One step
From the womb
Embraced
By the deep rapture
Of the slow eternity
I jump
From the belly of this bird
Like Jonah from the whale
Lazarus from the grave
REBORN!

Fort Bragg NC

Solider sweating in the sun
Clutching desperately
To my rifle and my rosary
Strangled by the conflict of faith and honor
So tired always tired

Contrived morality on the line
Soul for sale, body for rent
Deep rot of loss in the eyes
Confusion fear

Blood rushing roar

March to the next field of fire
My dog tags
Clenched tightly in my fist
Talisman and medals
Of my decision made

I think of home

Summer humid heat in the North Carolina forests
Artillery cannon roaring like thunder

FIRE MISSION
  ONE
  ROUND
  H.E. VARIABLE TIME FUZE
 SET CHECK
  LOAD
  FIRE

War paint running with sweat
Streaks my face with weariness
We prepare for war

I think of home

Bloodshot whiskey eyes
I sit alone at the bar
While the topless dancers
With pretty acid glazed eyes
And practiced plastic smiles
Seduce dollars
From lonely
Hard dick
Soldiers

I think of home

Drunken laughter fills the hallways
Loud
Full of brass and bravado
As the beer flows freely

Throughout time; only the flags change...

Dancing devils on broken angels
Do you hear the bells
Here comes the carnival
Body bag parade
Dressed in flags, honors, medals

And gun salutes

Walking through the paths
Breathing
Deeply of the still quiet air
Where nothing grows
Blanketed
By wreaths and thousands of little plastic flags
Whispering
In the wind thousands of names
All chiseled
With great care and sorrow in this Garden of Stone

Honorable Discharge; completion of service

Music drifts like smoke
From the radio
Hot summer rains falling
In this forested land
Boots
Polished to reflect like mirrors
Muddied by the wet grass.
This is the last time I will wear this proud uniform
I take a journey across the country
To leave behind my life,
To go to the real world
To return a stranger to my family, my friends,

I clutch my dog tags and think of home.

CHRISTMAS IN THE BARRACKS

Christmas in the barracks
A desolate place
Everyone gone on leave to be with family.

A green beer bottle pyramid for a tree
A tall glass
Of holiday spirits in my hand
My footsteps echo in the lonely hallway

Fayetteville is as silent as a stone
The sidewalks rolled up and put away
No neon shimmering in the tavern windows
Even the traffic lights sense the emptiness

CAMOUFLAGE NET

Netting...
Always the goddamn netting
And the buttons on my uniform...
Damn it all I hated the netting.
   Some devious drill sergeant going through a divorce
Again
               Had to of invented this shit.
   It's the only thing that makes sense.
Wrestling with the butterfly poles
      To push the net up
There's a twisted irony for you
Good to see that this engineer of hell
Had a sense of humor.

Unroll it off the back
Of the five ton truck
Everyone is cussing now
Three C130 jumps in two days
Ten or 15 hip shoots
That 155
Howitzer aint light goddamn it

Netting
Always the goddamn netting
Tangled all over fucking everything
All snagged up on
The legs of my girl
Pulling over her breechblock
There goes another damn button

Gonna be sewing for a week
The cleaners never get it right
And that's beer money

Net is up
Digging hasty fighting holes

Water...warm tepid water

A crumpled cigarette the last on the crew
Shared amongst four gun dogs
And
Always
    Always

The goddamn netting

    Whispering in the breeze
Promising more misery
Just one signal
 Away from another movement
To wrestle the net
And the butterflies
    In a hurry
The net the goddamned net
Can't we just leave that miserable bitch here?

Throw it in the back of the five ton
Gun hooked up
On the road to who knows when

And the net

The goddamned net

 Grinning pleased promised malice
  All tangled
And twisted
And knotted
Waiting
Patiently
Waiting

Like a water moccasin

Like the angry wives at post

To strike misery
Again
And
Again
Always caught in the goddamned net.

BAR FIGHTING WITH MULLETS

North Carolina 1995
I don't know if I
Ever actually
Hit the guy

My bell
Was already ringing
From the beating
I had took
But I remember swinging
For all I was worth
Before falling to the gravel parking lot

We ended up here fighting
With the local Mullets
After a disagreement
About a woman's marital status
Some women off post
Can be scandalous

I still carry a long scar
On my forehead
From where the fire extinguisher
Put my fire out

My right hand still
Has a large knot
Where the bones
Healed together
A little crooked

The next morning
Come first formation
I'll never forget Top
Looking at us
A battered lot
With pride on all our faces
And him saying

"At least y'all got your ass kicked together."

A FRIEND AWAY

Angel Face Rick was too cool-
A lone desperado
A super sleek outlaw
On the run
 A highway man
He liked that
 The romance of it
He could trace his family
Back to Jesse James
He'd like to brag
Between shots of scotch
And hits of cocaine
Swore he'd go down
Fighting
Like a man
Like a real movie mob gangster
He didn't

But he did go down all the same

JUNE 8TH 1996

So much undone
So many promises and vows
Like jagged glass and rusty barb wire

A demented dog from hell
Chasing its tail over and over

The terrible pounding at the door
In the house   pistol to the side of my head
Again and again
Beating my father
Gun at sister's and nephew's head
"Don't fuck with us or we'll kill the bitch and kid"
Ego tripping bad ass jailhouse tats
"Don't hurt them and I'll get you money"
Out of house into fathers Toyota
                              Family is safe
          No more fear overdosed on the fear
Sirens flashing lights
Gunshots
PAIN TERRIBLE PAIN

Gunshots flashing lights fading sirens

CHAOS FEAR
I DONT WANT TO DIE LIKE THIS
LIKE LITTER TOSSED FROM A SPEEDING TRUCK
PAIN TERRIBLE PAIN...blackness

A momentary lapse
I thought I was speaking
          To gods and saints in this morphine drip dream

So very strange my mind fragmenting through
This bloody prism of life
Turning my thoughts to confused nursery rhymes

             The wolf is at the door
                   Where is the woodsman
                   With his sharp and righteous axe
To split the belly and free me from these intestine shackles of
insanity

Pocket watches and rabbits...harmless
Insidious thieves of time

I wake up brutal and hurting
My face and body
A TWISTED
 Sculpture
Of broken bones
 Torn flesh
And FEAR
          My soul was captured
And forced back to my body
Cruel mockery of sacrifice
Promised freedom to be denied

                   I awake with my father's tears
                   Falling upon my bloody brow
Unashamed proud scared tears
                             I had never seen my
father cry before

PEELING

The peeling was the worst.

The peelings were the worst
Pain I have ever felt.

Nothing in my young 21
Years of life
Prepared me for the peeling.
Even through the morphine
There it was all brassy and loud and sharp
As each layer
Was sliced pried lifted pulled up
Peeled.

All the flesh on my face and arms and hands
And legs and back
Had been ground away.

It happens after being pistol whipped
Shot
And tossed out of a speeding truck.

When you hit the asphalt
At 65 miles an hour
It doesn't rip or tear
It burns
The friction burns the skin away
Cauterizes the flesh.

For three days
Twice a day
The orderlies would come in
Send the visiting family away
Bring out their knives and tweezers
And begin the torture
Of pulling the dead burnt flesh from my body
My eyes were so swollen
I couldn't even squeeze out tears
My jaw broken
I couldn't even cry out for mercy

Any mercy
Anything to stop the pain
To stop the sounds
Of my deadened flesh
Being pulled away
As if by vultures.

And they say I didn't die.

ONE BAD TRIP

My skin crawls like serpents itching and burning with poison
I'm lost
Won't someone help?
Compass gone mad, out here in the deep end
What thin new hell is this?
Lifetime of reruns between heartbeats
Shaking digs deep in the flesh
My hands won't quit trembling
Betrayed gone mad and strangled
Set on fire and locked within
Carnival sounds repeat dirge in the funhouse
Trapped within the warped mirrors of the mind
Christ bleeding laughs at me   steals my shadow   flays my soul
With barbed wire eyes of greed hate lust
Ashes in my mouth   ashes in my mouth
The palaces have crumbled
 Been crushed
The Slow Eternity is burning
The terror of it all   the cockroaches have taken rusty swords
And torches of pitch   no longer fearful of the light
Storming the walls   shuddering gasping breath
Awaken slowly   to rise   ruination
Bright screaming world   newborn   and covered in blood
My cries fall like lead leaves on deafened ears

Back alley abortion of my soul
Roman rape with a splintered cross
        All I have ever believed
        Now before me taunting hypocrisy
        Self-induced abusive illusions

Of peace
Of being a better man
Like a fluttering bird trapped and gone mad
Bruised and battered in this prison of glass

DEAR GOD JUST LET ME DIE

He laughs down upon me-   all that I was   nothing now
Renamed
MOCKERY   upon my brow…
The cockroaches burst free   cast aside sword and torch
Grinding mandibles they begin their feast
        This can't be real

GREAT SHIT ASS LYING MOTHERFUCKERS

Throw me away   discarded and broke
More litter along the road
I lay curled up in the corner
Eyes squeezed shut
Hands at my temple
Hands on my cock

Lunacy a welcome distraction

Is it over?   Or has it just begun?

I KNEW A WOMAN ONCE

I knew a woman once
Liked to quote
Gone with the Wind
Lots of drama as she would declare

I will never be hungry again

As she laid on the couch
With her Pomeranian
Eating two different kinds of potato chips.

Her real compassion
Would show
In the pleasure
She would take in others hardships
And the glamour pictures of herself

Lining the hallway
    Like the entrance
    To some sacred shrine
    To
    HER

Sometimes she would fancy herself a witch
Light a lot of candles
Talk about magic
And the
TRUE NATURAL WAY
While burning holes in the carpet

It was in the mail one day
In December
That I had found true freedom
With the signed divorce decree

CONTEMPLATION

The razor draws
Hesitation
Across the wrist of indecision
As self-aware contemplation
Takes over
Disguised
As
Something to live for.

THE SHOW

So here we are
All my clothes in black trash bags
Out in the front yard
Pages of notebooks waving in the wind
Left lying
Where you threw them
There's your little brother
And all seven
Of his friends
Waiting for me on the front porch.

We both know you don't want me to go
This is all just drama
Just another Tuesday afternoon soap opera
And you're just waiting for the show

So here we are
Back seat of cop car
Fire trucks lining the block
All the neighbors out to see
The fire jump out the windows
Of the house of love that we
Just burnt to the ground
Nothing left
But wet
Ashes
And ambulances
Rolling away like the final credits
At the end of our movie

TELLING LIES

You caught me
Trying to fuck around
With your friend
My ex

We got to arguing
The way we used to
Dishes and curses
Thrown at each other

You breaking pictures
Me punching holes in the drywall
You high on your drama and pills
Me high on my pride and booze

It surprised me
That the dumb whore
Called the cops

To be honest
I forgot she was there
I was busy explaining to you
That it wasn't my fault
That the little slut
Was a lying bitch

Your daddy and momma and little brother
All showed up
While I was
Shackled up
In the back
Of the squad car

Watching between the heart beats
Of the flashing red and blue lights
As
You and your family
Packed up
All your things

Beanie Babies
And
Glass unicorns
Photo albums
Cd's and VCR tapes
TV and stereo
A handful of "FUCK YOUS"
And a quick bird
Dumped the rest of my beer
In the dead flowers
Lining the yellowed yard
Took both the cars
And left...

The deputy asked
Me
Why
I was laughing

So I told him

We're gonna be doing this again
Come next Friday night
When I get paid again
When
She gets sick
Of her parents
Again.

SICK OF IT ALL

So sick of hurting all the time
Sick of being treated like a criminal
Sick of always going to court
Sick of this goddamned divorce
Sick of it all

Sick of having a P.O.S. for a ride
Sick of not having any money
Sick of bills I can't pay
Sick of doctors and surgeries
Sick of my family
Sick of hearing it could be worse
Sick of it all

Sick of Los Angeles
Sick of wanting to leave
Sick of believing the grass is greener
Sick of all the well-meaning cliché
Sick of my attorney
Sick of her attorney
Sick of not having a phone
Sick of having no one to call if I had a phone
Sick of it all

Sick of having to get drunk and high to sleep
Sick of Robotusin and NyQuil
Sick of hydrocodone
Sick of lonely morning hangovers
Sick of the news
Sick of the sunny weather
Sick of the traffic
Sick of it all

BOILED CHICKEN

I'm hungry
I should eat

But instead
I light
Another cigarette
And open
Another beer.

The man on the radio says
The future is uncertain
And the end is always near.
He also says
You cannot petition the Lord with prayer
Damn...
Always Aces and 8's
When playing solitaire confinement

It was at the Atlantic Market
On Atlantic Blvd.
Just north of the 91 freeway
When I meet Christ
Or Loki

(Depending on how you see these kind of things...)

In the form of an older black woman
With laughing eyes and gray hair

Years like testimony
Lined her face
Crinkled with a smile…

She told me how to cook the chicken quarters
I was buying
5 bucks for ten pounds
It was a good deal.

I wrote down
Every word
Of her sage advice…

I had been eating boiled chicken
Burnt rice
And undercooked beans
For months.

CROWDS

I pull the hood low
Over my eyes
Trying hard
To hide

Panic attack
Head turned inside out
Merry go round disco ball of thoughts
Scattered like broken glass

Hands sweating
Teeth clenched and grinding
Right eye twitching
Heart rate machine gun beating

Gotta get away
Find somewhere dark small and safe
Gotta get away
From the misfire synapse
Neuron traffic congestion

Take the medication
That's what the doctors say
Chemical lobotomy
There has got to be a better way

I pull the hood low
Over my eyes
Trying hard
To hide

DESPERATION

I want to be hung
On the refrigerator
Along with the rest
Of the children's
Happy drawings

I want to be the
Broken back field mouse
In the owls talons
Or the shaking needle
In the skinny junkies
Northridge Earthquake
Arm of collapsed veins

I want to be the donor organ
Two minutes too late
I want to be the tears
After crib death

I want to be the cancer cells
In the bone marrow rotting away
I want to be the ghost pain
Of missing limbs

I want to be the desperation
Of the last failed suicide attempt

CLICK

I write poetry
About suicide
Because
I'm to chicken-shit
To drop the hammer

Again.

See, I tried
Had a solid piece
.357 MAGNUM
Ran Federal Hollow-Points
Same as Secret Service
Quality ammo

The hammer fell with a dry final
      CLICK
That was the saddest sound
I had ever heard
At the time.

So I sat there
In my wheelchair
      24 years old
And crying like a baby

Had a young wife and a good job
Had a good pickup
She had a fancy sedan
6 horses and a ½ acre of land
Talks about children
$49,000 thousand a year
A full slice of the American Dream

And I'm told
By all the doctors
By all the specialists
Ten miles of college sheepskin
To tell me
That I'd never walk again
       And my last act
       As a MAN
       Ended in failure
I went a little mad that day
Things just didn't seem the same
Like waking up a GOD
The one eyed man
In the land
Of the blind

THE FRONT YARD OF MY MIND

The front yard of my mind
Is littered
With worn plastic lawn ornaments

Faded pink flamingos of lust
Little yard gnomes of pettiness
Bone dry bird bath of inspiration

Broke down Chevy of motivation
Engine compartment home
To the yard mice of yesterday's memory

And here and there in little patches
Tufts of green grass grows in the barren dirt
Little spots of hope taking root

24 HOURS ON A GREYHOUND TO DENVER

I had just got back
To North Long Beach
From Idaho
When she suggested I go
To Colorado
And see Angel Face Rick.

So I bought
An open ended ticket on the bus
To go to Denver.

I never realized how very long
24 hours can be.

At Vegas we stopped for an hour
I hit the saloon and the liquor store
With three pints snugged away
I figured I should be able to make the trip
With some peace of mind.

I'm all the way in the back of the bus
That seat no one ever wants
Right next to the damned bathroom
That never seem to work right.
Doors won't latch or there is no paper
Or no light
Or the constant fear of something splashing...

So there I am by myself
Quite content with a plug of chewing tobacco
And my illicit pints of sanity
Leaving the promise of Vegas
In a glow cutting through the desert night

I've got a grand little buzz going on
Half ass reading
Part of a newspaper
I found under the seat
And wondering what effect
The altitude there
A mile up in Denver
Has on the booze and women.

WHY I LEFT

Sometimes
It takes everything
Getting all strung out
     Twisted,   convoluted
Like the Los Angeles freeways
All jammed up
HURRY HURRY SLAMBRAKES
Mindless frustration
Of forward progress
Like being in love with a bi polar
Always hoping   looking desperate for that lane change
Fuel gauge dropping like empty depression
Temperature gauge screaming havoc ugly red
The
Pounding
Stop
 Go
Lurching
Keeping pace with horns
Calling fuck you
Punctuated with extended middle finger symbolic cock thrust forward
In emotionless rape of civility
As the enormity
Of our despair
Sinks back into my eyes

PART 4:

9 YEARS ADRIFT

FABLED EXCESS PATH

Exiled here on the Roads of Excess
Lost in search of
Those fabled Halls of Wisdom
Or maybe the path
Changes for each traveler

Here we raise our drinks
To the crawling Sun
Within it, a cruel promise of another
Sultry night to come

Washed gently in wine
We pull ourselves up
Vine by vine
To gather in Great Communion
Here at the taverns and Pubs
Where we engage in friendly unfamiliarity

All trying to find the quickest way
Into the Slow Eternity

7 DAYS A WEEK

The goddamned wrench slipped
Off the rusted nut
Slapping across the top
Of all ready swollen knuckles
Split open like a maniac grin
Blood like drunk laughter wells
Up deep and rich
Exposing bone and tendon

Hand wrapped tight with duct tape
Soggy sandwich for lunch
Wet cardboard taste
Stale cigarette
Ten minutes in
And called back off the break

To go back
To breaking back
And nuts
Trying to bust
Rusty nuts
Off this broken down wreck

A SIMPLE TRUTH

I ended up getting published
In the Modern Drunkard Magazine
By accident.

I was stone drunk at my normal chair
At the Streets of London Pub
In Denver
I was coming off
One of them good breakups...
You know
The one
Where you hate each other
But still end up drunk
And back in bed alone with each other
 After the bars close down
And everyone else has gone home...

So anyways; I'm trying to make a go
For the bartender
I figured I'd be clever
And throw down some drunk poems
Right on the spot...

I knew I scored
When she read them.

My feelings were mixed
When she told me her fiancé
Mr. Frank Kelly Rich
Former Army Combat Ranger
And father of
Modern Drunkard Magazine
Would probably publish me.

So Frank…
That's how my first poems
Came across your bar top.

TYPEWRITER RIBBON

830 on a Sunday morning
Drinking Jack and Coke
Waiting for the poem
To reveal itself
When the ribbon
On my typewriter went out...

Where do you find typewriter ribbon
At 835 on a Sunday morning anymore?

So now
It's back to pen and paper
And Jack and Coke
At 840 on a Sunday morning

SPEAK EASY TEA

Is that the sun I spy?
Like a shy child peeking over the Denver horizon
Never seen beauty quite the same
As I try to climb into the cab

A proud party we three make this night
After hours bounce, speak easy and remember the knock

What a glorious moment this night has become
Etched deeply, like the hand of God writing
        Into the halls of the Slow Eternity we wander

With bold hearts and strong drinks
Poured straight from heaven towards our glasses
Strained from tears and laughter

Or so I like to say when I'm feeling charming
At 6:00 A.M.
When the marbles have been washed from my mouth
And the introverted turtle shell has expired

Together we took our souls to the quantum moment
And washed them well in our whiskey
And hung them to shine like the gleaming brass of the taps
And together we reinvented the lost art of the salute

And a-stagger in the glorious sunrise
I feel my head becoming heavy and weary
And though I would want for nothing more
Than this moment to remain eternal
I feel the hounds of sleep nipping at my heels
As we mumble promises of another night like this
As we shamble off to our beds

WHITE LIES

She lays her head on my chest
Whispers in my ear
I just need you to lie to me tonight

So I tell her
I'll be here
In the morning when she wakes
That I'll be home before the sun comes down
I tell her that we will run away
One of these days

I tell her
I love her

She smiles and snuggles close
And whispers

Leave the money
On the dresser
On your way out.

DRUNK DIAL

"You're drunk"
I know
"Why do you call me when you are like this?"
I don't know
"You won't even remember this conversation."
That makes it all the better
A little easier
To swallow the squares
To eat the pride
And binge on the fear
"Why do you do this to me?"
I just want to make sure
That you are suffering
Still
The same
As
Me

TOY AISLE

29 years old and you can't
Take him to a store without
Him heading directly to
The toy section

All of a sudden

The ten year old he never was
Is all over his face

Climbing out his eyes
Jumping off the tire swing
Of his smile
Spread out like
An explosion of atomic
Memories of yesterday
All the things that
Could never be afforded at the time
When he was never ten years old

Hours spent staring
At little plastic
Idols and heroes
Mass produced avatars
Of grand mindscape adventures
That are 19 years too old now
To bring any comfort
To the ten year old that never was

With the same reluctance
Of any child to grow up
He walks away from the toy aisle
And heads to the liquor shelf
Two bottles
Of 90 proof self help
To help put
The child's things
Of yesterday away

DRUNK AND REMEMBERING DENVER JOE

I think I'm gonna open a bar
And
Call it
GRASSHOPPER
Wait wait wait…

That's someone else's drunken rant
I'm tripping
Who dropped my DNA on a sugar cube?
Expanding on a tongue
Opening a psychotic sink hole
That has swallowed me whole…

What are you trying to hear?

I mean

What are you trying to hear me say?

That you say
You heard me say
That I said
You said
I said
That I never said
That you said
Anything?

Deafest ears and draw the blinds...

Tie me off Uncle Dick
I think I missed
And will someone get my Aunt Lois
Outta the men's room...

Wait...that's Denver Joe's drunken rant...

But I'm getting closer

To what you say
I said
You said that I...

Aw hell...I'm lost again
And the Cricket on the Hill
Is just an old memory

AGREE WITH HER

You know I'm quite certain you've had enough to drink
She says
And I'm sure you've smoked enough cigarettes and weed
She says
Yeah…you're probably right
I reply
While she's opening another beer for me
While I light another cigarette
And inhale deeply
Then
I light another with the same match
For her
You know you're incorrigible
She says
You're always going to be a dirty white boy
She tells me
You're wasting time with that writing
She says
You're never gonna get anywhere with it
She says
      I drink my beer
And make no reply
As she looks down at me with contempt
You know I only say this because I love you
She says
Why don't you take that job at my daddy's shop?
A stock boy isn't a bad job
She says...

And I take a long pull from my beer
Wishing it was whiskey
Watching me slowly fade away
A pale imitation of what I was
And I think
About my upcoming suicide
Ending my life with
A regular eight every day
Home by five and watch TV
And eat bland gray food from colorful
Bags and boxes
And have a dog I hate
And some kids I don't recognize
Yeah...
I reply
While looking at her
As if an entire universe just came to be
And exploded
And all the light from the room drains away
And all the laughter on the radio fades
And all that is left
Is to drink
And smoke cigarettes
            Smile and plot my escape
And agree with her

PSYCH MEDS

I don't like these drugs
They don't do the tricks
Like the other one does

Smile big because we're all sick
Cause we're all searching for that new fix
Cause we all got something to run from
Memories of yesterday's past atrocities
Dirty feelings of guilt
Hung from the gallows
Hand built scaffolding to set the soul free
Count the steps to 12
Find the missing apostle
Head towards the chapel
Climb all the way up the steeple
Get away from all this babel
And fall
Fall all the way back down
Fall like a defiant angel
Fall like a Morningstar
To change the course of history...

I don't like this new drug
It just don't do it for me
Like the other drugs
The better ones
Poured from the cups of heaven.

ROLLER COASTER

Back and forth these emotions flow
Riding along on currents of tears
How I wish I could be more like you
So sure and confident nothing ever bothering you

Novocain heart and cocaine eyes
How I wish I could be more like you
Looking at the world through distant glass
Lives tumbled beneath you like TV reruns
No remorse or regret
 Or second thought to disturb your sleep

How I wish I could be more like you
To ball up my fist in your hair and throw you
Choke you slap you till you got right
Till you understood me
Till you wished you could be more like me
All fucked up rusty barbwire
And broken glass
Grinding bones constant pain
Broken and always hungry
Prowling the streets looking for the hustle
Anything it's gonna take...

How I wish I was more like you
Then I could do all this to you
And then we could
Always be at each other
Fucking fighting
All blurring together

So much passionate anger
Hard to tell the love
Apart from the hate
And we break each other down
And it's so fucking sick

You're such a stupid bitch you stay with me
And
I'm such a stupid bitch I stay with you

All fucked up and you punched me in the mouth
We ended up
Fucking like crazed beasts on the couch
And you hit me and bit me
I growled and pulled your hair and choked you
And you spit and screamed you hate me
And I covered your mouth
And fucked you harder
And you fucked me harder

Back and forth
We keep doing this mad dance
And back and forth I wish
I could be more like you

Cause maybe then it wouldn't hurt so much.

ME, CARLO ROSSI WINE AND BEANS AND RICE

Undercooked rice
And burnt beans
You'd think I'd have this figured out by now.
Cans opened with a screwdriver
Don't know what happened to my
P38
Mockery from another time
When I had a purpose
And a uniform
And a bed...

I really don't mind the cork floating
In my bottle of wine
But Carlo Rossi has been good enough
To provide a half gallon jug
With a twist off cap
So with a halfhearted smile
Of my own demise
Remove the facade
Undo the disguise
Hook the thumb hole of the bottle
Tilt up and admire the moon
Through the bottom of the jug
As I wash away memories
Of everything that was yesterday

Live forever immortal
With no memory
Of what came before me
No attachments completely numb

Safe within a room
With no windows and no doors
Each moment forevermore
An eternity between heartbeats
Back to the womb
Oblivion...

BACK MONKEY

Sunday morning coming down
On the radio
Eases past the hangover
Slow and warm
Like the crawling ant
Of a day getting underway.
Pick up the pieces
Of memory from the night before
Glue them back together with Crazy
Hope it holds
Long enough to get to the refrigerator
To get another beer to face the morning
To chase down the pills and cigarettes
To give the reach around
And scratch the back monkey behind the ears.

GRANITE FABRICATOR'S SONG

The dust gets every where

So fine it can burn

Powdery almost chalk like

Covering everything
Like passing time
And shrouds over bodies not yet risen

It builds up in your nostrils
Binding into hard plugs
It climbs and settles in the ears
Mixing with the wax to become as cement
Grinds away the fabric of clothing
Works into the pores turning skin to leather

Powdered glass slow death
The granite fabricator's
Every wheezing breath
Slow drown blood fills the lungs
SILICOSIS
All the while
The constant
Vibration
Of the
Makita variable speed grinder
Sings
The slow death dirge
Of
Granite and flesh

TOILET PAPER EPIPHANY

Two rolls of toilet paper
Hidden up each pant leg
Trying to walk normal
Clock out from work
Don't want anyone to know my shame
Work forty plus
Hours a week
And I still can't
Afford to
Wipe my own ass

IT WAS YOUR LAUGH

It was your laugh
That first got me
There at Burger King
"A friend of Bill; right Dude?"
You said to me.
It took me a moment
To collect myself,
There I was
On my way to the courthouse
With my ex- wife
To finalize the divorce.

Fortune does shine
At the oddest times

1.   **TO DO LIST**

2.   She was always making him To-Do Lists

3.   All those lovely little Honey Do's

4.   That'll drive a man's soul straight into the ground

5.   And he would always check those lists

6.   One by one like it was a rosary or something

7.   Helping dig his own grave

8.   One check point at a time I guess

9.   We both worked the night shift at the granite shop

10.   He would always show up in a jacket and tie

11.   Pressed shirt and shined shoes

12.   Like he was going to court or a wedding or a funeral

13.   Which is like going to same thing; no matter which one you're at

14.   Just really matters where you're sitting at the time I guess

15.   Anyways he'd show up like he was going anywhere but to grind granite

16.   He'd change in the men's room and go to work

17.   Real obedient about the time clock

18.   About his work pace

19.   How long of a break or lunch

20.   And always checking off his damned list

21.   I asked him once about the tie and jacket routine

22.   He never met my eyes
23.   Just kept reviewing his To Do list
24.   And explained
25.   That she required him
26.   To leave for work this way
27.   So as to keep the neighbors
28.   Unaware
29.   About what he did for a living

30.   She told everyone
31.   That he was a business executive
32.   For an international company
33.   And worked the night shift
34.   To account for time differences
35.   In other countries

36.   That sucks man
37.   You should change
38.   Your situation
39.   That's no way
40.   For any man to live

41.   I put out my cigarette
42.   Went back to work early
43.   While he finished checking off his list

44.   End of shift
45.   We both clocked out together
46.   As normal

47.   What was odd

48.   Was he turned
49.   Shook my hand
50.   And said goodbye

51.   That and he was smiling.

52.   In the years grinding with the fella
53.   I can't ever remember him smiling.

54.   And that was it
55.   I said goodbye to him as well

56.   The next night I clocked into work
57.   Millar wasn't there.

58.   On the break table
59.   Was his To Do list

60.   Everything was checked off

61.   The last two lines were what caught my eye

62.   Shake hands with my best friend and say goodbye
63.   Go home load gun/change my situation.

64.   His best friend?

65.   Damn, five years we worked together
66.   We maybe had three conversations
67.   And two of them were about work
68.   I'm not so certain that qualifies as a best friend

69.   That's when the foreman came in and said
a.   Did ya hear?
b.   Millar went round the bend
70.   Went home and killed his wife and himself
a.   I never saw it coming
b.   Not from that guy he was so straight laced

71.   Yea I know I replied
72.   He was wrapped up pretty tight
73.   And I walked off to the shop
74.   To grind granite

AA MEETING

The chairs were uncomfortable
And in different states of despair
Same as the broken mass of people
That were sitting there
Styrofoam cups full of overcooked coffee
33 stories
Of misery
Of recovery
Of promises revealed
Of roads trudged and travelled

SERENITY

Detox
30 days kicking
Sweating puking
Shitting shaking
Clueless in the rooms
NEWCOMER first day
Nothing making any sense
12 STEPS
Stumble through the fog
Trying to find a *PORT OF HOPE*
Or the *LAST HOUSE ON THE BLOCK*
Needing something to hold on to
Willing to go to any *LENGTHS*
To find a *HIGHER POWER*
ACCEPTANCE
POWERLESS
Makes you powerful
In the *MIGHTY PRESENCE OF PEACE*
Worries and cares lifted
As if by a *GREAT WIND*
Blowing down from the *MIGHTY MOUNTAIN*
The *KEYSTONE* the glorious *ARCH*
Of *SERENITY*

ME AND JIM

Me and Jim were both drying up
Two booze hounds
With tail tucked between legs
And hands still shaking.
He had a month on me in sober time

I had just lost my father
And my job
 And then I gave away my mind
I was in a deep spot.
He took me to my first AA meeting
Then on Thursday he took me
To meet the **DOGPILE MEN'S GROUP**

I spent that first month
Kicking blankets sweating sin out
While bills piled up
And the world went insane
…I was in a bad way

That November
Jim noticed all I had to wear
Was my working rags

He ran me down to the Wal-Mart
To get some new clothes
Without stains or holes

Clothes that a man
Can interview
For a job in
Shoes slacks
A blue shirt black tie
And a belt
Jason's wife Rachael cut my hair
I shaved my beard
And scraped the dirt from under my fingernails

34 days sober
Looking like a new man

LEAVING SERENITY

Being sober
It's a lot like being hungry

It's easy
When you just
Don't think about it
Or fill your gut with anything
Other than what you really want.

The thirst wasn't too bad for me when I went dry
It was
Always the meetings
And the greetings
And all the social interactions
Meaningless distractions

And it was enough to drive me mad

All the constant yak yak
Who's doing who/what/how/why
Back in jail or back relapsed
Yak yak
Cigarettes glow in the falling Idaho snow
And everyone is still running on
About who has how much time
Or what step they are on
Or how humble they are

And it was enough to drive me away
And I became enough to drive me away

All the hypocrisy
All the ego tripping bullshit
And how addicting the podium could be
Worse than the thirst
The attention I craved
Up on that wooden stage
Preaching to the broken and depraved
A tribe of my own kind
But somehow I was gonna be better

Look at me
Look how coolly I walk away
And leave
Serenity
Behind me
Jumping back
Headfirst
Into my own Mouth of Madness

FOOD BANK

Standing in a long line of shame
A disabled combat vet
And his wife
Guiding him
On shaky legs and cane
Her arms to support and steady
The years collected in the gray of her hair
The lines on her face
The curled worn hands
That have tended first his mother
To the end
And now him
With what bit of dignity they have left
His proud ball cap Vietnam Vet
Her proud husband at her side
His weekly outing
To collect a cruel box of food

SEVEN YEARS IN IDAHO

Sometimes I get so bound up
With the need to stand up
Raise my chin in defiance
Open my mouth
Ready to yell something
But
Out comes nothing
Head lowered
Eyes cast to the side
As I remember why
I need this job
Counting to ten
Again and again
Till the 330 whistle
Sings mercy
Clock out quick
       Before
I can get caught
And chained down
Again
With mandatory overtime
Off the clock
That I can't refuse
Cause the power bill is late
And the damned rent is due...
       Come home
She's still in bed
       Thorazine dream walker
Lithium lady

                    My wife
Slowly sinking away   farther and farther
New prescriptions
          Seroquel   Abilify
Depakote
          Black box medications
I brush her hair
Out of her face
          The medicine makes it thin
I make her something to eat
Put on a new anime DVD for her
Set the player to repeat
Shower do laundry
Clean house
                    Lock door behind quietly
Go to bar
Bill n Lynn's
The Whitewater
All night
Glass never empty
          She sits down next to me and says hi
          Her hand upon my leg
          Knowing lust in her eye
I sink back a glass of lonely
And order another;
As I pop down two methadone tablets...
I don't want to remember
What's going to happen next

EVERYONE IS ALL DRUNK AGAIN

Everyone is all drunk again
While I'm looking deeply
Into the eyes of my bourbon

Bill N Lynn's bar
Low lights and wood panels
Tired singing jukebox
And a wobbly pool table
With 7 balls

Everyone is all drunk again
While I'm looking deeply
Into the eyes of my bourbon

There goes Ben
With the karaoke heart break again
Jessica is out for another fella tonight
She's out for a good time
She's got time to kill and a bed to fill
Her old man just took a pinch
Got popped for distribution
Riding low with a kilo
Picked up a nickel at IDOC

And everyone is all drunk again
While I'm looking deeply
Into the eyes of my bourbon

Thoughts lost
On my wife
Who is
Lost
Caught
Up in a psychoactive
Medicated stupor
Another open ended stay
For mental health observation

I brush her hair from her face
Hold her hand
Lie again and say it's going to be all right…
She sees me leave my wedding band
On the hospital night stand
Just before I leave…

And here I sit staring deeply
Into the eyes of my bourbon
All drunk again

A soft sanctuary of oblivion
Knowing I'll never return the same man
I finish the bourbon
And take my turn
On the slow suicide
While Ben sings
Big Bad Leroy Brown

DONT CHASE THE CIRCUS

Here it comes
Like dark clouds
Crawling in from the ocean
To crowd the shoreline

Can't you hear the carnival music?
The acrobats are out walking the wire
The clowns are in the car ready to go
This is my freak show life

Why do you ask?
Why do you always ask?
Why are you always so surprised?
You knew I was only going to lie
You knew all I was ever going to do was lie…

SPRING CLEANING SALE

Like a Lion
I got a letter in the mail
Said 50% off
Spring Cleaning Sale

It was addressed
To current resident
So I left it
There on the empty
Kitchen table

Walked down the hallway
Past all the condemning portraits
Dead faces
With no voices left
To mock and heckle
Me on my way
Out the door
Like a lamb

IT'S COMPLICATED

I just couldn't help myself
Some the things
That fell out my mouth
Some of the situations
I have found myself in
Complicated emotional positions

It'd be funny if it wasn't true
But it always ends up
With the same questions
From the "this time"
Different
Version of YOU
That I find in front of me

Again
Asking
Screaming
Crying
Pleading

Why don't you talk to me?
Let me in...

And I just couldn't help myself
Some the things
That fell out my mouth...

PART 5:

20 YEARS LATER

18 YEARS

It's like seeing family and friends
After being gone for 18 years

Lakewood

Hawaiian Gardens

Long Beach

Los Angeles

So familiar

But I'm really

Just a tourist
In my own memories

And the old neighborhood
Is still there
With the same streets
I ran wild through

And the streets
Still sound the same
And the streets
Still smell the same
And the streets
Still look the same

And the drunks on the corner have stayed just the same

And the same Mexican
Pushes the same tamale cart
Down the same street
He did 18 years ago
Except now he's old
Probably has a wife and some kids
Probably a car payment
And a mortgage or two

And the neighbor lady is still there
Still yelling
At the neighborhood kids
Goddamn
I think those
Are the same damn cats

And the house where the girl
Who I lost my virginity to
Is still right there
In the middle
Of it all

It's like seeing friends and family
After being gone for 18 years

Everywhere I've been
There's nowhere
Been anywhere
Quite like here

Now I sit on the porch
In this beautiful backyard
At that same house
Waiting for my woman
To come home
So we can walk
Through the old neighborhood park
And ease the night away
With good dark beer
And memories
And stories
Of the last 18 years

POETRY READINGS AND AA MEETINGS

Poetry readings
Are a lot like
AA Meetings
Filled up
With all sorts
Of screwed up people
Up in front of everyone
Spilling emotional
Guts
Heart felt confessional
Of survival
And dips into madness
And how you came out the other end of this
And of course there are the girls
And the opportunity to re-invent yourself
And everything comes down to time
How long have you been slugging away
Doing it just like
Everyone before you

WALKING THE LAKEWOOD MORNING

At the corner
I see OK Liquor
Where
The last Pay Phone
Stands lonely guardian
Of yesterday's communication

Turn right on Centralia
Walking slow up the hill

605 North and South beneath me
A bridge over a busy sea
Of steel and light

The tires slapping the asphalt
Sounding just like the ocean

While the Sheriff's Nosey bird
Spotlighting my neighborhood
Sirens crying down Pioneer
Crossing Carson into the Gardens

Low sea fog creeping like a stalker
Through Rynerson Park
Perfect cover
Broken
By the glow of my cigarette
As I follow the San Gabrielle River north
Mind crowding
With the Ghost Song
Of Fabled Failed Youth

Swinging back down the Del Amo hill
Heading back to the 208th
Past Haskell
That's the Jr. High
Where I spent
The first half of 7th grade
And the last half of 8th grade

Past Del Taco and the donut shop
That used to be Mi Amore's Pizza

Roll south on Pioneer
Remembering when Omega Burger
Used to be Dukes
Where we used to meet
Coffee and cigarettes
Before first period
At Artesia High

Back on 208th
The Street is just coming awake
Cars barking with the dogs
Nosey Bird chased away
By the rising sun
And green parrots

I fall to my bed
Remembering the names of yesterday...

WEDNESDAY MORNING

Sirens rape the morning quiet
A life ending
A life beginning
Maybe a cat in the tree
Or another kid stuck in the concrete river
>   But the dogs don't much seem to mind
>   Undeterred in their mad quest for invisible cats and possums
>   And sunbathing bellies in the yard...
I envy them at times
The simple honesty of being a dog in the summer...
Another draw off my cigarette
Another pull off my beer
>   I've taken to smoking light filtered cigarettes in a brief
concession to age
>   I still remember the non-filtered hand rolled smokes
>   Tobacco on the tongue and the cheap harsh burn
But it's still good
It's enough
It gets me through
Like when she just looks at me and smiles
Not saying a word but so much shared
And I find myself like the dogs
Tail wagging running in circles in the summer sun

BANNER MARKET

Banner Market
It's just an empty lot on Centralia now
Burnt to the ground
A few years ago

Like so much else

Another landmark of my life
Gone away
Without preamble or eulogy
Just an empty space
Surrounded by a sagging chain link fence
Over grown with weeds
And old memories

DRIVE SOBER

All that I wanted
Was someone to drink with me
Wouldn't you know my luck
I finally found you
And you're crazier than me
And it looks
Like the same old rat race
Of sitting in Los Angeles traffic
Trying to merge the 5 to 101
At five in the afternoon…

It's good that you
 Are a married woman…

You are the sort
To drive a man sober

HOME

Monday morning driving
K-Day mixing it up in my speakers
Tattoo and CC taking me
Down Carson
Left on Los Coyotes Diagonal
Driving with my knee
Loading another bowl
Pull the toke
Load lungs with the smoke
Before I run the traffic circle
Roll right onto PCH cross past Atlantic
Long Beach Blvd coming up
Train stops everybody looking
Strollers walking the street
Players and gangsters
Broke ass bums
Dirty faced children
Pay day loan
Bring in your title
 Get your paper
Moving on over the river
Left on Santa Fe
Deep in industrial park
Harbor big trucks   containers everywhere
Cruise back to 710
Loop around   fight across to the far left
Head for 405 to 605

Dropping onto Carson
Long Beach to my left
Hawaiian Gardens on my right
Fall up to Norwalk
Chase the memory of Artesia High –Cutting-School
To Palms Park
Smoking cigarettes
And small twisted joints
Sipping half pints
A lifetime ago
A generation ago
Left onto Del Amo Blvd
Remembering when everyone had to front
Everyone wanting to be down and hard
Left back on Pioneer
Heading home
Forever East Lakewood
East Lakewood Forever

HUSBAND FATHER FAMILY MAN

And I don't know what I'm playing at
Not sure I'm cut out for this

Still dreaming about the freedom
Of the open road and nowhere to go
The freedom of the hustle

And I don't know what I'm playing at

Dreaming about putting the gun
Back in my mouth
Step right up to the bottles
Pain pills and Jack Daniels
Drop back insane again
Mumbling to myself
Reclusive vagabond
The whole world beneath my feet
What little good memories that are left
Carried in a rucksack
Keep moving to the next nowhere
To the next broken heart break up
Keep moving to the next spot to stop
Keep moving or get rousted by the cops

And I don't know what I'm playing at

Never had it so good as I have it today

Husband father family man

And I don't know what I'm playing at

Supposedly my drifter ways
Were left with the yesterdays
So why do these thoughts
Keep coming to haunt me
Why does the road keep calling to me
Siren song of promised misery
Found in the useless miles
On the useless hi-ways of life
That have already been travelled?

And I don't know what I'm playing at

ONE OF THESE DAYS

It's been 3 years now
Since you passed.
You would've been 62 today...

We had always talked about doing it
For years upon years
And it was always one of these days.
And we sincerely meant it
A solemn vow between us

We talked about doing it
At Denny's the morning I left for the Army
We talked about it
In the backyard the first time I got married
And it was still one of these days.

It was when going through my first divorce
You and I
Took your little red Toyota pick up to the Kern River
Fishing poles in back.
It was a hot July
Not even the mosquitos were biting
You taught me to drive a stick shift
We talked for hours under beautiful stars
Passing smoke around the campfire
And for one weekend
It was one of those days
We finally did it...

We were father and son.

87 OCTANE

Groaning morning
weary rising
sunless day
Broken by dog
barking
bitter coffee
 gurgling
Cigarettes
smoking chains
While pills popped
chase away pains
As old cold blooded pickup
Coughing to life
mimicking my rusty lungs
Belching blue smoke rings
Of 87 Octane
Rich
with the sweet smell
of unspent fuel
Like the ghosts
of the dreams
from last nights
slumber
Rich like the dreams of
youth

LONG BEACH HARBOR

(2013 Joe Hill Poetry Award Recipient Poem)

Bellowing of ships horn
The low constant rumbling
Of heavy trains grumbling
Away
Of new products and labors born
Steel rebar and concrete
Sinewy muscles
Contract moving
Groaning bone protests
 Another building
Growing into the skyline
Connected together
By freeways
And bridges
And streets and alleys
And sidewalks and bike lanes
Glued together by endless flow
Of cars and trucks and trains and planes and people
Like blood pumping through the body
Seized with coronary traffic congestion failure
Of the human heart
As another work day
 Bleeds
 To
An end

1972 C10

Looking at a picture of you
Tomorrow so far away
Long memories lead my mind astray

Plans of a future together on the road
Chasing the wind
The radio singing those old travelling songs
Solid 70s gold
Keeping tune with the singing of the tires
Eating the miles up one after another

Right arm across the bench seat
Around my girl
Left arm crooked out the window
Holding the wheel
A cigarette smoldering in my lip
Speedometer holding a steady seventy

On the 91 highway on a Saturday
Heading back to the beach
Following the route
My father used to commute
To pull oil from the wells
Down in Signal Hill
And Venice Beach
Back when this old pick up
Rolled off the assembly line new

PARANOID

I sleep with loaded weapons.

I walk the house checking doors and windows.

I set traps in my yard at night.

I have read many instructional/military manuals
On survival

I memorized the Anarchist's Cookbook.

I know all the manifestos.

Even wrote one of my own.

Everyone calls me paranoid.

Tell me to go back to my mountains.
Tell me to go back to my deserts.
Tell me to go back to empty hi-ways

But I know the truth
I hear you in my house
Crawling in the attic
Trying to be quiet as the mouse
All the while peeking at me
Watching me
Hiding behind the pictures on the walls
Smiling at me from behind smiles frozen in time
Waiting for me to slip
Waiting to slither your insidious way into my head.

Everyone calls me paranoid

LESSON IN MORTALITY

Three loud pops
Like bundles of rubber bands
Snapping
Releasing

My bicep is gone
My fore arm
Knotted up like the roots
Of an old tree stump

The pain sweeps
Like a December Pacific wave
Full of menace and undertow
Throughout my whole body

Everywhere at once
Every nerve screaming

I am incredibly cold

Shock

Sweat from every pore
The hurt is sickening
A constant blow to the gut
For the first time
In a very long time
I am afraid

DAY JOB

So you're a poet huh.
And you've even been published you say.
Did you get paid for it?
No huh.
So maybe this week
You'll spend a little time
And write a pretty little ditty
About how you went out
 And found a real job.
Quit being a child
Time to put the crayons and coloring books away
Put on some work boots
You do remember those
Don't you?
Maybe come home
With a paycheck and maybe some benefits huh?
See this is what happens when I leave you in charge
Last year
Homeless
 Sleeping in the car
Pick up work day labor
We lost thirty pounds that winter
Remember the hunger?

Nah, we forgot all about that
Didn't we you sissy summer grasshopper
Lay about moaning about
Being a writer
Trying to make a break
While I'm out busting my nuts and breaking my back
Running every hustle in the book
Trying to get something to eat
Trying to find somewhere dry to sleep
While you're jerking off that ink pen
Keeping us up chasing dreams
When we should be sleeping
Or out hustling
Or looking for a day job
To quit
Before we jump off the cliff.

A DOG DOWN

I think he knew
The hammer weighed heavy in my hand
 Like a guilty conscience
A rifle would've been better
Cleaner...somehow removed.

I think he knew
Between the tumor
And the infected wounds
It was time. Past time.
Couldn't watch him suffer anymore
The hammer weighed heavy in my hand
Like a guilty conscience

I think he knew
He was a little dog
My swing was true...

I buried him gently
Then confronted the mirror
To wash the tears and blood off my face.

BUTTERFLY KISSES

Butterfly wings
Your breath against my ear
A tsunami
At the other end of my heart
Santa Anna wind
Against my skin
Your fingers
Explore our original sin
Together
An ocean meeting the shore
Fire leaping from wood
Singing in the trees
Flight of birds explode
From within consciousness
Awareness
Your scent so very near
Eyes dilate open wide
To give birth to mind
Images of your smiles

LISTENING TO CLASSICAL MUSIC WHILE DRINKING A DR. PEPPER

Symphony No. 9 in E minor

I really don't know what that means
Only that's what the description says

Only to be changed to
The Swan Lake
Which to me
Just sounds
Like emotional scenes
From Star Wars movies

Images of memory
Splicing together
Like reels of film
Flashing behind the eyes

Grand anticipation
Subtle climax

And the music
Gets deeper and heavier

Instruments I never heard
Making sounds that stir
The heart and mind...

It's just a shitty recording
Playing through
Some tin can sounding speakers

But still

Each piece of the music
A different flavor

Riots of color invading my ears
My soul lifting higher
Than the smoke exhaled

As it all
Slowly
Fades
Like the old picture tube T.V.s
Dropping to a single point
And
Then
Gone

SERENADE

I was gonna write you a poem
But my auto pen
Wouldn't quit laughing
I was gonna sing you a song
But the auto tune
Wouldn't quit laughing
So I still screwed up the courage
And crept through the night
As quiet as a brick through lead glass
Fell over the backyard fence
Landed in the hedges flat on my ass
Thorns pricking my skin
The way your eyes ripped through my heart
Walked up to your window
And began to sing
With the stray cats keeping harmony
While your dog howled and bit my leg
Chased me through the yard
Back over the fence
Dog ran me all the way down Pioneer
Cross Del Amo and into Gridley Park
Thought I lost him at Haskell Jr. High

How wrong I was
How surprised
To hear his heavy panting on the back of my neck
Teeth gnashing at my heels chasing me all the way
Back down Del Amo turn right on Pioneer
Back over your fence
Quiet as a brick through lead glass
Fall into hedges past the startled cat
Flat on my ass
To catch moonlit glimpse
Of you in your night time window
Laughing at the singing fool
Running circles
Chasing your dog's tail

LISTENING TO YOU

I love listening
To you talk
Watching your lips
Move seduction
Across your teeth
Over your dancing tongue

I get lost
In the shimmer
Of your eyes

As your hands move
Creating beautiful worlds
For your words to live in
Inviting me
Tempting me
To jump in
Head first
To drink deeply
To answer the burning thirst

MORNING COMMUTE

And the wind
Blowing from the cracked window
Of the passenger side of the truck
Against my arm and cheek
While we hurtle along the freeway
Diesel motor growling its cadences
As the miles churn away
Like frothy waves
From the bow of the boat
That was a memory of summer long ago
Your skin golden brown from kissing the sun
Your hand in mine in front of the camp fire
The catamarans resting on the shore
Bullfrogs singing throaty lakeside songs
Your head on my shoulder...

Shattered by the blaring of air horns
Grinding gears
And screaming brakes

SENTENCE PASSED

Sentence passed
Condemned
To life in a chair
No chance of parole
That's what
The Devil
Disguised as Fear says

So everyday day
Looking out the front door
At the life passing by
He stares
And remembers
When he was younger

Out running the streets
Chasing skirts
And barking at the moon
Shackled up Road Runner hot rods
Two tours in Viet Nam
Raising children
Taking care of business

Six foot six
Tossing a shadow
For lesser men to hide in

        Somewhere
        Deep inside

Smoldering

        Are the embers

Turning

        To fire

Guided by his faith
Led by this light

        Each morning deep into his Bible
        He studies the plan
        He plots his great escape
        From this chair

Looking out the front door

WITNESS

There is no dignity in dying
It's always the same
 No matter how different
We all die
Most times we piss and shit ourselves
And cry out
In pain
 Anguish
Or fear.
Seems to me
 If you're really lucky
There's a morphine dream drip
 Going on
In a chemical coma
Just waiting to burn out
With no one
To witness
The room
Go dark...

OLD PHOTOGRAPHS

I go to look at old photographs of us
They're all that is left now
It hurts to look back
And see all that can never be again...
Pictures of you and me in the pool
I must've been about nine or ten
Diving off your shoulders;
You throwing me like a cannon ball
Sister swimming around like a minnow with arm floaties
8th grade at medieval times
Sitting in thrones wearing paper crowns
There we are when I graduated high school
I had never seen you in a tie before
And here we are, I'm home from basic training
Pictures of a proud father shaking his son's hand
My first wedding you and me in tuxes
You were my best man
You were always my superman

And then
Like always
Like every time
I come to the end of the book
The last picture I have of us
All your children and grandchildren
Gathered around you
Your eyes still bold and daring and proud
2 months
Before the cancer slowly took you away
Leaving only photographs
All that's left
Of what will never be again

BULLHEAD CATFISH

A parade of awareness
Slow march behind the eyes
While my father's face
Carefully watches me from the mirror
As I shave   slow and steady
As he taught me

                    He was always meticulous
                    About his appearance
                    Cutting paths
                    Like the grass
          Between tombstones
Me and my cousin Tony
Drove him up to a little pond
For one more fishing trip

                    Along with everything
                    The Cancer took away
                    From him
                    The Kern River

We didn't have any bait
But we sat out a pole for my Dad
Opened up beers   opened up souls
Spread tears   and memories
And his ashes

The pole bent low
We reeled in a big
Bullhead catfish
Out of that pond

I LIKE

I like cold beer
And good rolled up homegrown
On a Sunday afternoon
After mowing the yard

I like the way my dog
Clamps her teeth
On my hand gently
To reassure me.

I like the way
The winds and rain
Rolling off the mountains
Or deep breaths
From the ocean
Clears away the sky stains

I like the way
Lynard Skynard sounds on the radio
Turned down low
During the night time settle

I like coffee at 430 in the morning
With my woman
Before the rest of the world is awake

LISTENING TO JOE COCKER

Listening to the music
That my father enjoyed

Trying
To better understand him

I suppose this is one of those journeys
That will probably never end

Constantly looking to hear him
Laughing in the wind

Trying
Again and again

To remember
Every word
Every gesture
Every moment
Shared together

SHAMBLE STUMBLE SLOW SHUFFLE

Two broken people
Nothing left but each other

Down the sidewalk
Shamble stumble slow shuffle

Hand in hand
Nothing but each other
Like a rusted plow
And a weather beaten barn

They stop
As he kneels
Upon unsteady knees
And ties her shoes
First the left then the right

While slowly gaining his feet
Her crab apple face splits in a smile
That reveals the beauty
Hidden beneath the miles
Takes her hand in his again

Shamble stumble slow shuffle
Down the sidewalk

Heading up Norwalk Blvd

He says
Voice creaking
Like a dry leather saddle

We're almost there
The doctor gonna have the fix

And I got cotton mouth
And am sick too honey

But I got the spoon
And you got the harpoon
And before you know it
We gonna be dancing on the moon

Shamble stumble slow shuffle

CEREAL

I hit the inhaler
 So I can breathe
I smoke the weed
So I can keep peace
I smoke the cigarettes
Cause I'm too lazy to quit
I drink the booze
To ease the physical pain
I eat the pills
To jumpstart the morning

It's like
Jerking the dog off
To feed the cat
To eat the rat
To keep the cereal
In the box

TOM WAITS AND WARM BEER

Listening to Tom Waits
And nursing a warm Corona

Too many cigarettes
Too many scratches

The cd skips cd skips
Cd skips

Like my thoughts skip
Like smooth rocks
1, 2, 3, holy shit!
Four times
Across
The pond of yesterdays
Future
In a spinning bottle
And a Magic 8-ball
In a temple
Chasing dragons
Through the smoky pagodas
To burst like new birth
Into a sudden world
Hidden with all the missing socks
And all the lost change in the couch cushions
Right next
To all the discarded dreams
Of youth

IT ALWAYS GETS SCREWED UP

It always gets screwed up
When it gets personal
I prefer
The detachments
When I'm degrading you
When you're degrading me
I don't want us
To be people
Someone we might care about

I prefer when we are not real
So when I show you
How worthless you are
With my mouth on your cunt
When you show me
How worthless I am
With your mouth on my cock
We will know it's not personal
We are both just getting off
Bringing each other
To the lowest common denominator
Both bottomed out
Jump off the edge
Lost in the grunting
And the rutting

FUNERAL

Cut hair shave beard
Polish shoes
Put on suit and tie
Go to the church
Say goodbye

Hug relatives I don't know
Say nice things
To people I'll never
See again.

Service over
Everyone gathered
Eating food
Talking quietly
Compliments
On the bacon and green bean casserole
And how pretty the flower display was

Back behind the trailer
A joint passing around
Cans of Tall Boys
Passed around.

This is the only time we ever get together
And even then it's rare

I maybe stay an hour or so
Before I find
I'm ready to lose my mind

A good enough
Reason to have to go
Get away from all this false family
Circling vultures

So I pay my respects
Finish my brew
And head back to the freeway

Last can of beer
Between my knees
As I shift through
The mental gears
Sifting through
All the past years
While I race the falling sun
Back to the ocean

37 YEARS OF MEMORIES

It's hard on her
He's gone
Almost 5 months into memory
And she don't know what to do
With all the empty space and time

37 years all gone
37 years of everyday

One way or another
Always tending to someone
Always not enough time for her

Now
Engulfed in empty time and space
I watch her
Helpless
As she drowns in the emptiness
Trying to find her balance
Trying to remember

And it's so very hard on her
All the old comfortable conversations
Sitting on the porch together
Reminiscing
About 37 years of memories
Inside jokes and hopes and dreams
All gone now ashes to ashes
And quiet late night tears

And I'm helpless
To help my mother
As I sit here in my own hell
Drowning in my 37 years of memories

A NOTE ABOUT CELEBRITIES

Generally you'll find yourself
Disappointed
When you come to see
That star you've been wishing on
Is really nothing more than debris
With momentum
Flashing across the screen
To quickly burn out leaving nothing behind
But wreckage.

ON POETRY CRITICS

I've heard it said
You're only as good
As the last thing
You wrote…

Makes sense
Seeing as
The last thing I wrote
Was a hot check
For groceries
And beer
And a quick stop at the
Pot dispensary

SOME DOGS DON'T HUNT

Some dogs don't hunt
I said to him

We were talking about the poetry scene

I was mostly trying to absorb
As much knowledge as I could
Trying to glean wisdom
From this old dog
Long in the tooth

But I kept finding myself distracted…

I mean it is not often
That you get
To pick the mind
Of yourself
Twenty years later
On/Off the Beaten Path
That was the road not taken
By me

This time…

My mind drifted to theories
Of alternate realities

While stoned

We laughed
 About poets
And his new discovery
Of
String Theory

CELL PHONE

I despise the mobile phone.
I try to explain
This to people
But it seems like
People have trouble understanding
That I'm not tethered to my
Mobile phone

I miss the days
Of a rotary phone
Set on the end table
Dial O for operator
Or the wall mounted
Push button phones
Hung up in the kitchen
With the 25 foot cord

I miss watching TV on the television set
I miss listening to the radio on the stereo
I miss sending letters on paper through the mail
I miss ignoring the blinking light on the answering machine

I miss being able to ignore the phone
Take it off the hook
Or un-plug it from the wall
I miss
When I'm not home
You have to
...Leave
Your name
Number
And a brief message
At the beep
And I will call you back.

TRYING TO MAKE IT

Trying to force a poem
Is
A lot like
Trying to make a screw
With a broad
That's just as bored of you
As you are.

All the moves are there
You know all the right words
But the spark
That wet moment of success
Never comes

HOMESTONE

The world looks better
With dark sunglasses on
Everything muted a little

Not so bright
Not so harsh

A measure of protection
If I can't see them clearly
They can't see me clearly

Here
Covered in tattoos
With beard and clothes
As stringy
And greasy
As my personality

Everybody stay away from me
Leave me alone
Where the hell is my woman?
Damn it I want to go home
Everybody talking too much
Everybody too bright
Too loud
Too colorful

Can't any of you see?

There never was a Captain America
Superman is a lie that will die
And dreams are the whip
To keep you compliant
As sheared sheep

God help me
God hang me
God damn it

I spent all the rent
Again
At the bar
Slowly with gin

And I still can't find my woman
My salvation
My hearth where I hang my heart
The rock I cling too in bad storms
My Home Stone

THE END OF THE LAST POEM

The end of the last poem
Will begin
With a
Bullet
Car wreck
Heart attack
Cancer
Marriage divorce
Death
Birth
Life love

The end of the last poem
Will begin
The same as it ends

Like DNA
Twisting spiral connected
Like cell division
Like the splitting of atoms
The opening of the universe
In one thought
A little spark

AN OPEN LETTER TO ANY WHO WILL LISTEN

See there is a whole other AMERICA that lies beneath the
surface.
Everybody likes to talk about it
Act as if they know about it
They like to say what's wrong with it
They like to breed dissent within it
Keep us fighting amongst ourselves
Never looking at what's going on behind the curtain
Blind sided with knee jerk emotional appeals disguised as
legislation
That only furthers
Their own Robber Baron agenda
Of social enslavement
Keeping the people
Hungry tired angry poor distracted
All the while
Contently vomiting Orwell nightmares
Thru the eyes and into the head
Keeping the brain numb and immersed in shit
Tamed and complainant
With constant streaming live feed media input
Immediate gratification buy now consumerism learned
stupidity disguised as entertainment

And we have failed.

Poets and bards
Had been the front line troops
For every revolution
Of social reform
Always there

Spreading the word
Sharing the reality the degradations the experience
Until now.
We have failed our calling
We have failed the poets before us
We have failed our heritage of DEFIANCE
We have failed ourselves

Used to be
It was dangerous to be a poet
To express
New and undisguised ideas
Road weary voices
That called for change
Endured the loneliness
The ridicule and disdain
The beatings and jailing's
For violation of
Murky and obscure obscenity laws
The hunger
The addictions
The drunkenness
The madness
The brawls
The sex
The suicides
The lonely dying
And the fear   always the fear
gnawing at your mind
Like hunger crazed rats...
Where are our Bukowskis?

Who will be our Blake?
Our Rimbaud Baudelaire Verlaine?
Where the fuck is our Kerouac
Our Ginsberg and our Whitman?
Where is our Poe?

Where is our Fear?
Where is our VOICE?
Where is the defiance?
Where is the **GODDAMNED DEFIANCE**!?
RAISE UP
Embrace that motherfucking god-head defiance that makes
poets
That drives us
To madness and addictions and every other experience
That we can possibly suffer
To flood our minds with
That defiance
That makes us say to the masters
No. **NO MORE! I WILL NOT GO QUIETLY! I WILL
NOT SUBMITT!**
To raise our voices   to wash away the stench
Of all the dddddouble talk fine print
Political head spin doctors weaving
Honeyed nightmares of mind killing nonsense

Are we so lost?

Have we no star to guide us
No witches or shamans
Has the mount become insurmountable?

Or do we come together
As a guild
A union
A legion of voices
Do we catch the fear?
Ride it
Feed from it
Grow from it
Learn from it
Teaching each other to become it
Do we sing our defiance while birthing
Challenging thoughts of change?

Or do we lower our heads
And bleat with the other sheep
Awaiting the sheers
And then the butcher?

DOG LESSONS

When I want to know
How I should act as a human
I look to the best example
Possible

I watch my dogs intently
Everything they do
Is by instinct

It seems to come so easily
Naturally
Why can't we
Make better effort
To treat each other better

Maybe instead of handshakes
For greetings
We should look to the dog
Smell each other's ass
To have a better appreciation
Of each other's experiences
To know well each other's burden of shit

J. W. Gardner is an Army Airborne Veteran and a 2nd Generation American drifter and writer who calls East Lakewood, CA home. More nights than not he can be found at home, enjoying the comfort of his family and his dog.

Joe is the Founder and hired gun for *Working Class Production*, as well as creator and co-producer of *The Last Sunday, An Evening of Poetry and Art.*

He is also the *2013 Joe Hill Labor Poetry Award* recipient and his work has appeared in *The Modern Drunkard Magazine, The San Gabriele Valley Poetry Quarterly, Cadence Collective, Spilt Ink Poetry and AMASS Magazine.*

He has also been published in the following anthologies:
Gutters & Alleyways: Perspectives on Poverty and Struggle
The Men's Heartache Anthology
Lummox Anthologies, 1 thru 3.
Edgar Allan Poet 3

The LUMMOX Press publishes

Chapbooks, the Little Red Book series, a perfect

bound book series (the Respect series), a Poetry Anthology &

Poetry Contest (annually), and "e-copies".

The stated goal of the press and its publisher is to

Elevate the bar for poetry, whilst bringing

The "word" to an international audience.

We are proud to offer this book

As part of that effort.

For more information and to see our

Growing catalog of choices, please go to

www.lummoxpress.com/lc

www.ingramcontent.com/pod-product-compliance
Lightning Source LLC
Chambersburg PA
CBHW022121080426

42734CB00006B/206